Saxon Math K–3 Placement Test

Introduction

If you are uncertain which level of the primary materials to use, the first criterion to consider is the child's age. The following chart should be used to determine the recommended instructional level:

Age	Level
4½ – 5½	*Math K*
5½ – 6½	*Math 1*
6½ – 7½	*Math 2*
7½ – 8½	*Math 3*

AF830690

Exceptions

If a child has significant learning problems or has received little or no prior math instruction, consider beginning at a lower level than what is recommended on the chart.

If a child has received prior math instruction and you consider the child's ability and understanding of math concepts to be exceptional for his or her age, consider administering this primary placement test to determine whether the child should begin at a higher level than what is recommended on the chart.

Directions for Administering the Primary Placement Test

- This is not intended to be an end-of-the-year test, and it should be used only with children who have not previously been in a Saxon mathematics program.
- Administer the test to one child at a time in a quiet, calm environment. You may wish to have someone else present to record the child's responses and comments.
- Read through the questions and prepare all materials prior to beginning the test.
- Follow the instructions and dialogue on the following pages. Answers are shown beside the questions.
- Depending on the answer, the child will receive 0 or 1 point for each question or set of questions. (See the boxed numbers.) Add the points at the end of each section for proper scoring.
- Before beginning, explain to the child that this is an opportunity for you to find out what the child already knows.
- **This is not a teaching situation.** Do not correct the child when he or she responds incorrectly or provide hints when the child hesitates. Record the child's answer without indicating to the child whether the answer is correct. Praise the child for focusing on the task and listening carefully.
- Begin with Part A of the Placement Test. At the end of each section, read the directions to determine whether to continue.

Part A

materials
Master P-1 (Cut apart the box of shapes, the number cards, and the paper strips.) 20 pennies, 2 nickels, 4 dimes

1. Identifying Shapes

- Point to the square from **Master P-1.**

"What shape is this?"

- Repeat with the triangle, circle, and rectangle.

Correctly identifies all shapes:	1
Incorrectly identifies one or more shapes:	0

2. Counting By 1's to 100

"Count as high as you can."

- Stop the child at 100. The child's last correct number is ________.

Counts to 100 correctly:	1
Cannot count to 100 by 1's:	0

3. Counting Objects • Matching Sets of Objects with 1-to-1 Correspondence

- Place 8 pennies in a row. Leave space between the pennies.

"Make another row of pennies that is the same as (matches) my row of pennies."

"How do you know that your row is the same as (matches) mine?"

"Count the pennies in my row."

"Count the pennies in your row."

Uses correct number of pennies:	1
Uses too few or too many pennies:	0

Counts pennies correctly:	1
Counts pennies incorrectly:	0

4. Matching Sets and Numbers • Ordering the Numbers 0–10

- Put 20 pennies in a pile on the table.
- Show the child the number card 7.

"What number is this?"

"Show me this number of pennies."

- Repeat with the 9, 3, and 0 number cards.
- Give the child the number cards in a mixed pile.

"Put these numbers in order."

Uses correct number of pennies for all cards:	1
Uses incorrect number of pennies for one or more cards:	0

Orders numbers correctly:	1
Orders numbers incorrectly:	0

Part A (continued)

5. Identifying Coins • Sorting • Identifying Most and Fewest

- Put a penny, nickel, and dime on the table.
- Point to each coin and ask:

"What do we call this?"

- Put 6 pennies, 2 nickels, and 4 dimes in a mixed pile on the table.

"Sort these coins."

Identifies all 3 coins:	1
Identifies 2 or fewer coins:	0

- If the child does not know the meaning of the word *sort*, say the following:

"Put the pennies in one pile, the nickels in another pile, and the dimes in a third pile."

Sorts coins without assistance and answers all questions correctly:	1
Unable to sort coins or answers one or more questions incorrectly:	0

- Allow time for the child to do this.

"How many dimes do you have?"

"Which coin do you have the most of?"

"Which coin do you have the fewest or least of?"

6. Measurement

- Place the strips on the table in the following way:

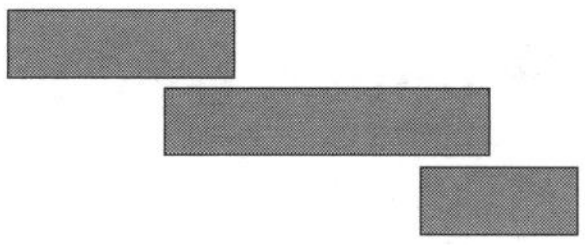

"Which paper strip is the longest?"

"How do you know?"

Identifies the longest strip:	1
Identifies an incorrect strip:	0

- Remove the two shorter strips of paper.
- Give the child 20 pennies.

"How many pennies long is this paper strip?"

Measures accurately by placing the pennies close together:	1
Leaves wide spaces between the pennies or does not complete task:	0

Total Points Part A: ________

If the child scores 8–10 in Part A, give Part B of the assessment.
If the child scores 0–7 in Part A, stop here and begin with *Math K*

materials

Master P-2

Calendar of current month
7 pennies, 3 nickels, 6 dimes
Ruler with inch and centimeter scale
Pencil

1. Identifying the Date and Days of the Week

- Show the child a calendar for the current month.

"What month is it?"

"What year is it?"

Answers all questions correctly:	1
Answers one or more questions incorrectly:	0

- Point to today's date on the calendar.

"This is today's date."

"What is today's date?"

"What day of the week is it today?"

"What will be tomorrow's date?"

"What day of the week will it be tomorrow?"

2. Counting by 1's, 2's, 5's, and 10's

"Count by 1's, beginning with 80."

- Stop the child at 140. The child's last correct number is ________.

Counts from 80 to 140 by 1's correctly:	1
Cannot count from 80 to 140 by 1's:	0

"Count by 2's as high as you can."

- Stop the child at 20. The child's last correct number is ________.

Counts to 20 by 2's correctly:	1
Cannot count to 20 by 2's:	0

"Count by 5's as high as you can."

- Stop the child at 50. The child's last correct number is ________.

Counts to 50 by 5's correctly:	1
Cannot count to 50 by 5's:	0

"Count by 10's as high as you can."

- Stop the child at 100. The child's last correct number is ________.

Counts to 100 by 10's correctly:	1
Cannot count to 100 by 10's:	0

Part B (continued)

3. Counting Money: Pennies, Nickels, and Dimes

- Put 7 pennies, 3 nickels, and 6 dimes in a mixed pile on the table.

"How many dimes are here?"

"How much money is that?"

- Repeat with pennies and nickels.

"How much money is this altogether?" (82¢)

Identifies coin values correctly:	1
Identifies coin values incorrectly:	0

Counts the money correctly:	1
Counts the money incorrectly:	0

4. Identifying the Missing Numbers and Shapes in Patterns

- Give the child **Master P-2.**

"Read the first pattern out loud."

"What are the next three numbers (shapes) in this pattern?"

"Write (draw) these numbers (shapes) on the lines."

- Repeat with the next three patterns.

9, 8, 7, 6, ___, ___, ___ (5, 4, 3)

5, 10, 15, 20, ___, ___, ___ (25, 30, 35)

6, 16, 26, 36, ___, ___, ___ (46, 56, 66)

△, □, □, △, □, □, △, ___, ___, ___ (□ , □ , △)

Completes all patterns correctly:	1
Completes one or more patterns incorrectly:	0

5. Measuring and Drawing Line Segments

- Hand the child a ruler. Do not indicate which scale to use.
- Point to the line segment in problem 2.

"Use the ruler to measure this line (segment) using inches." (4")

"On the back of your paper, draw a 3-inch line (segment)."

Measures correctly:	1
Measures incorrectly:	0

Draws the line segment correctly:	1
Draws the line segment incorrectly:	0

6. Telling Time to the Half Hour

- Point to the first clock.

"What time does this clock show?" (10:00)

- Point to the second clock.

"What time does this clock show?" (8:30)

Identifies both times correctly:	1
Identifies one or both times incorrectly:	0

Part B (continued)

7. Identifying Fractional Parts of a Whole

- Point to the square in problem 4.

"Divide the square in half and color (shade) one half of it."

Divides/shades one half correctly:	1
Divides/shades one half incorrectly:	0

- Point to the shaded circle in problem 4.

"How much of the circle is shaded?" (one fourth)

Identifies fractional part correctly:	1
Identifies fractional part incorrectly:	0

Total Points Part B: ________

If the child scores 10–13 in Part B, give Part C of the assessment.
If the child scores 0–9 in Part B, stop here and begin with *Math 1*.

Part C

materials

Master P-3

5 quarters, 5 dimes, 5 nickels, 5 pennies
Ruler with inch and centimeter scale

1. Writing Numbers • Adding Using Mental Computation

- Use the back of **Master P-3**.

"Write the number 47."

"What is 1 more than 47?" (48)

"Write the number 16."

"What is 1 less than 16?" (15)

"Write the number 35."

"What is 10 more than 35?" (45)

"Write the number 83."

"What is 10 less than 83?" (73)

Answers all questions correctly:	1
Answers one or more questions incorrectly:	0

Part C (continued)

2. Counting Money: Pennies, Nickels, Dimes, and Quarters

- Give the child 4 dimes, 3 nickels, and 2 pennies.

"How much money is this?" (57¢)

Counts the money correctly:	1
Counts the money incorrectly:	0

- Give the child 4 quarters, 10 dimes, 10 nickels, and 10 pennies.

"Show 17¢ using the fewest coins." (1 dime, 1 nickel, and 2 pennies)

"Show 65¢ using the fewest coins." (2 quarters, 1 dime, and 1 nickel)

Shows both money amounts using the fewest coins:	1
Uses incorrect coins or does not use the fewest coins:	0

3. Reading a Thermometer

- Point to the first thermometer on **Master P-3.**

"Color this thermometer to show 30 degrees."

"What temperature is shown on the other thermometer?" (36°)

Colors the thermometer and identifies the temperature correctly:	1
Colors the thermometer or identifies the temperature incorrectly:	0

4. Identifying the Missing Numbers and Shapes in Patterns

"Read the first pattern in problem 1 out loud, and fill in the missing numbers (shapes) in the pattern."

- Repeat with the next three patterns.

Completes all patterns correctly:	1
Completes one or more patterns incorrectly:	0

21, 23, 25, 27, ___, ___, ___ (29, 31, 33)

45, 40, 35, 30, 25, ___, ___, ___ (20, 15, 10)

___ ___, ___, 47, 57, 67, 77, 87 (17, 27, 37)

 ___ ()

5. Measuring and Drawing Line Segments

"Use the ruler to measure the line segment in problem 2 using centimeters." (10 cm)

Measures correctly:	1
Measures incorrectly:	0

"On the back of your paper, draw a 4-1/2-inch line (segment)."

Draws the line segment correctly:	1
Draws the line segment incorrectly:	0

6. Telling Time to the Nearest Five Minutes

- Point to the first clock.

"What time does this clock show?" (2:25)

- Point to the second clock.

"Draw hands on this clock to show half past one."

Identifies both times correctly:	1
Identifies one or both times incorrectly:	0

7. Identifying Fractional Parts of a Whole

- Point to the square in problem 4.

"Divide the square into 4 equal parts."
"Color three fourths of the square."

Divides the square into fourths and shades three fourths correctly:	1
Divides or shades the square incorrectly:	0

- Point to the circle.

"How many parts is the circle divided into?" (8)

"Write a fraction to show how much of the circle is shaded." (3/8)

Identifies fractional part correctly:	1
Identifies fractional part incorrectly:	0

8. Reading a Graph with a Scale of 10

"The graph in problem 5 shows last week's high temperatures."

"What was Wednesday's temperature?" (20°F)

"On which day was it the warmest?" (Thursday)

Answers both questions correctly:	1
Answers one or both questions incorrectly:	0

Total Points Part C: ________

If the child scores 9–11 in Part C, begin with *Math 3*.
If the child scores 0–8 in Part C, begin with *Math 2*.

Cut apart the box of shapes, the number cards, and the paper strips.

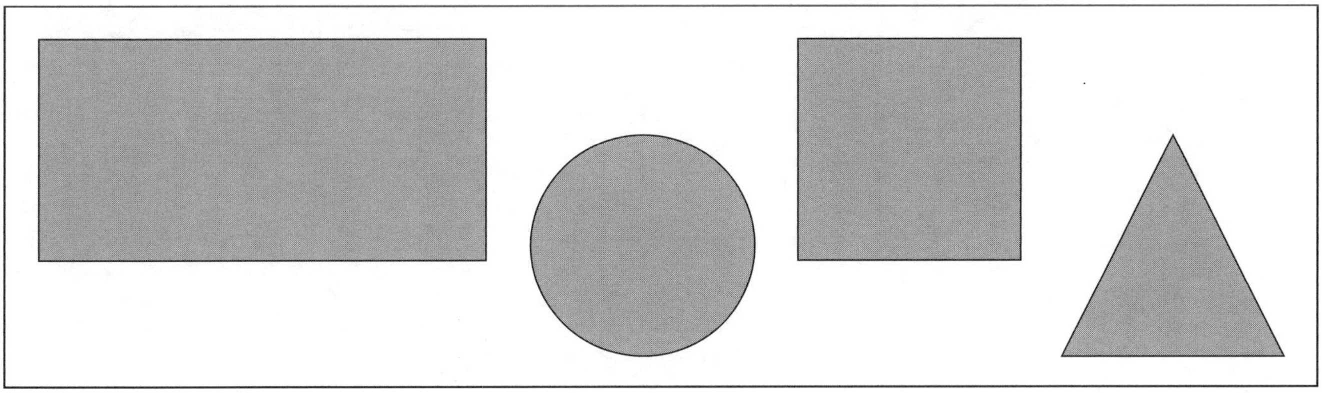

0	1	2	3	4
5	6	7	8	9

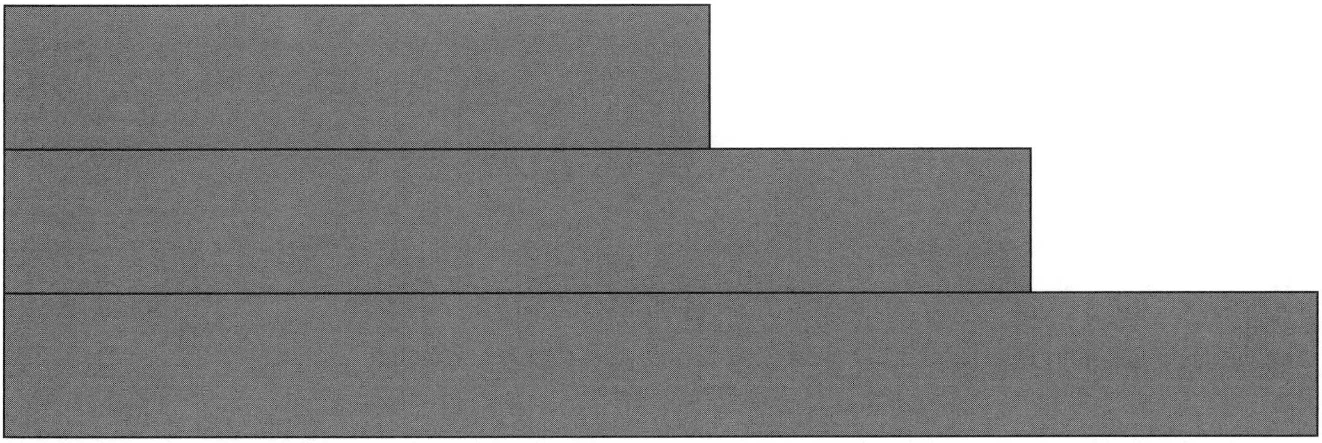

Name ______________________________

Date ______________________________

K–3 Placement Test
Master P-2

1. 9, 8, 7, 6, ____, ____, ____

5, 10, 15, 20, ____, ____, ____

6, 16, 26, 36, ____, ____, ____

△, □, □, △, □, □, △, ____, ____, ____

2.

3. 

4. 

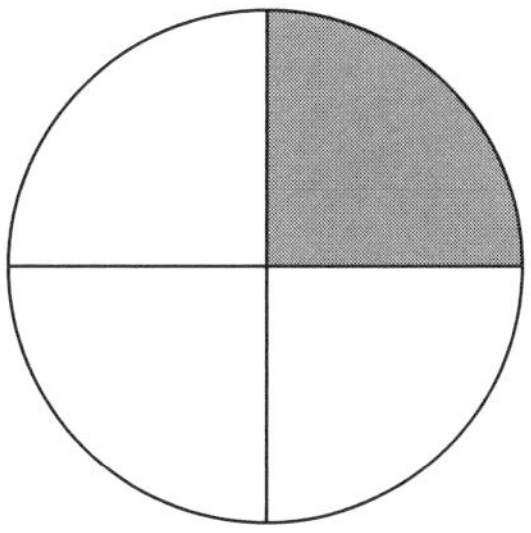

Name ______________________________

Date ______________________________

K–3 Placement Test
Master P-3

1. 21, 23, 25, 27, ______, ______, ______

45, 40, 35, 30, 25, ______, ______, ______

______, ______, ______, 47, 57, 67, 77, 87

, ______

2.

3.

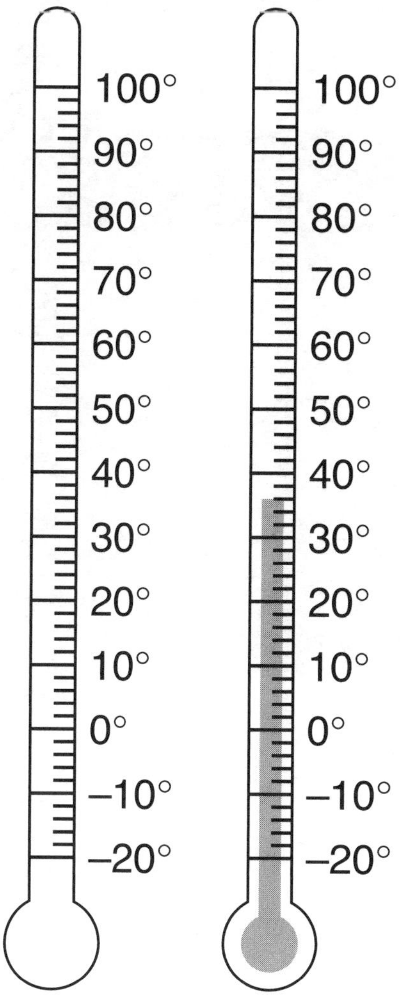

4.

$\frac{3}{4}$

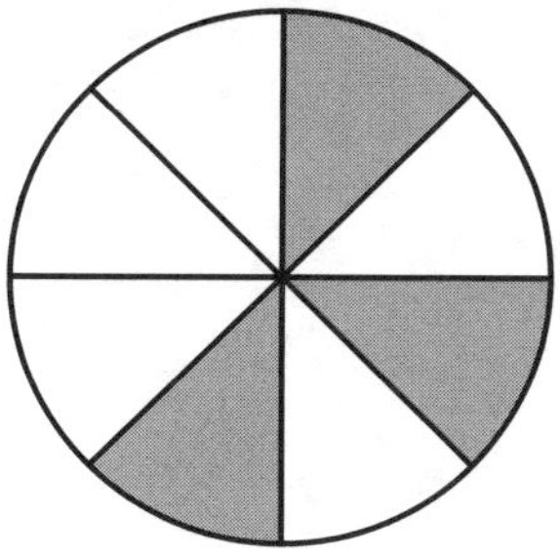

5.

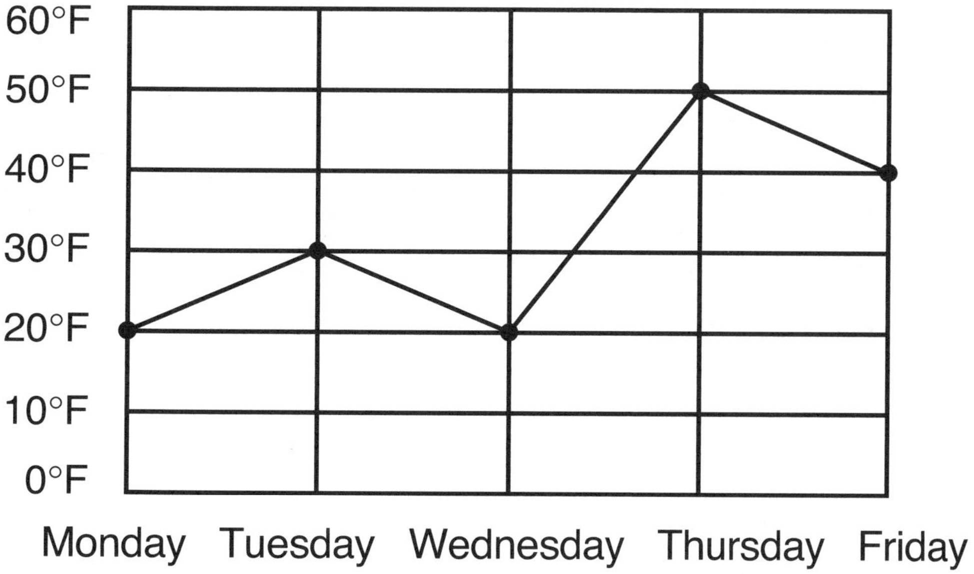

SAXON MATH™

SAXON™

A Harcourt Achieve Imprint